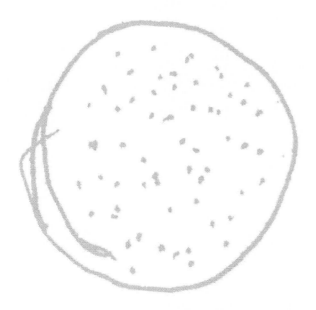

Body Clock

POEMS

Eleni Sikelianos

COFFEE HOUSE PRESS

COFFEE HOUSE PRESS books are available to the trade through our primary distributor, Consortium Book Sales & Distribution, www.cbsd.com or (800) 283-3572. For personal orders, catalogs, or other information, write to: info@coffeehousepress.org.

Coffee House Press is a nonprofit literary publishing house. Support from private foundations, corporate giving programs, government programs, and generous individuals helps make the publication of our books possible. We gratefully acknowledge their support in detail in the back of this book. To you and our many readers around the world, we send our thanks for your continuing support.

LIBRARY OF CONGRESS CIP INFORMATION
Sikelianos, Eleni.
Body clock : poems / by Eleni Sikelianos.
p. cm.
ISBN 978-1-56689-219-3 (alk. paper)
1. Motherhood—Poetry. I. Title.
PS3569.I4128B63 2008
811'.54—dc22
2008012529

PRINTED IN THE UNITED STATES
1 3 5 7 9 8 6 4 2
FIRST EDITION | FIRST PRINTING

ACKNOWLEDGMENTS
The author wishes to thank the editors and publishers of the following magazines, anthologies, and calendars, where some of these poems first appeared. *Joyful Noise: An Anthology of American Spiritual Poetry, Not for Mothers Only: Contemporary Poems on Child-Getting and Child-Rearing, American Hybrid: A Norton Anthology of Contemporary Poetry, Poetry Calendar 2006* (Alhambra Publishing, Belgium), *Onedit, Coconut, Conjunctions, Chicago Review, Colorado Review, Tarpaulin Sky, MoonLit, The Portland Review, 580 Split, Plan B, Drunken Boat, Mantis, Parcel, Origins, Not Enough Night, English Language Notes, Copper Nickel, Free Verse, 26,* and *Typo.* A section of the book appeared as a chapbook from Bonfire Press.

Thank you also to my editor, Chris Fischbach and to my lovely live-in editor, Laird Hunt. To Selah Saterstrom, for help even in the swamp. To Susie Schlesinger, Emma the Sheep, and Brown Bag Farms, where I was afforded some of the most beautiful hours. And to the vast and growing community of poets, writers, and readers (living and dead, in this country and in others) who keep this thing going.

D'Arcy Wentworth Thomspon's *On Growth and Form* was an inspiration in the beginning stages of this manuscript. Other authors, books, or texts that are quoted in the poems herein include John Bulwer (from *Chirologia: Or the Natural Language of the Hand,* included in *Imagining Language*), Walt Whitman, Giorgio Agamben, Tomaž Šalamun, and Anne Carson.

This book is for Eva Grace
(for now, and for when she can read)

"of spatial magnitude, or of the extension of a body in the several dimensions of space"

"Growth involves the same concepts of magnitude and direction [as] . . . the 'dimension' of Time"

—D'Arcy Wentworth Thompson

CONTENTS

heart was
found   asymmetrically
locked in the chest   You can't make it
turn round   not around

_____

pierce the
porous skin of
a minute   see time bleed out
_____

THE SWEET CITY

UNTITLED (THE GARMENT OF PRAISE)

Put on the garment of praise
    Boy and Girl of praise Joy
Move god on the lips

Joy or luck fell into a swoon
a barrel of light
sweet crude

an agent having power
to reduce, destroy, or consume

Oh here comes a doggess sciomancer divining love
and hate by means of shadows and clouds

a beautiful bitch communicating with
ghosts of the living and dead

Sunlight falls across the body
      The house creaks, inspiration hits

      What are we doing here? All
our movements and actions
are helping or hindering
the dead

THE SWEET CITY

Then I came back   and it was still October. The city

        was still in flames. The lead
        rolled over us like light. Every second
        the city's particulars
        changed. The city will
        edit itself & adjust or the city
        will   more
        than any single   eye   can
        see. The stationary and moving
        parts. The names remained
        to be listed and named. I lay down. How definite
        is this bed? And the body that lies in it? I am thinking
        something outside is
        infinite, what? A blue thing, a thing blue
        that has existed for a week, a thing blue
        that has existed for a day. It makes sense to say
        about someone that she was for a moment   happy

Blue, o blue thing   be more good with all
gooder things that are

Perceptible black, perceptible blue that the world contains
If you want to see the lights of a town go down
go to New York. If you want to see smoking holes and buildings bristling
out of Baghdad's back take a train to Brooklyn.

Wake up to the story of fire,
Student of nature,

the once uncuttable atom
will touch you now.

✝

          the grace of arms & legs
silkening through other rooms

✝

✝

the whole round night is drowned and alive;
black Palmetto bugs hiding
from porchlights under porcelained leaves
will make it

through the dark halls of cryptography,
nanotechnologists of the celled night

          in us: 100 trillion tiny containers,
apartments for vacant lots / thought & makings
of vacuoles

charred & pulverizable

What thoughts of the night
or a day do you bear cutting into deep muscle
to carry this rippling, waves riding out the darkened bay
A city's spinning mouth o's smoke rings, city hit

with life, light hitting the skin, wind
or water moving over limbs
as they too move, gifted gestures of casual symmetry

                              hands how
                    hands
              How many
hands move down a
day   Down
a day

One ball of the finger to count the eyelashes (ash)

Bullcart the eye, drag a mess past
            the retina into the brain
Now what can the mind do but
                be carried along by it

+

There will be time to lean on things of the day
    Pleasure boats float   and school buses line up, yellow metacarpal
        matchboxes with no momentary children   Manhattan bristling in the back
        ground still

+

rags hang on the tumbling wire
stretched across the river, fluttering fingers emptied of what   It
eludes me, but
significant, too, are spiderworks on
iron gears for opening floodgates
Everywhere I look, human
endeavor: This lake
was made by a man who paid men
to dig it.   The canals, too,
were shoveled by men who died at it.

     Out in the fake lake
the Great Blue Heron moves not an inch—I know
we've built some design on it—
     walking, flying, fishing, fighting machine—
        powered wings, graceful legs
    (born in the mind of some workman)—

☩

      they began by tearing up trees then founded
          break points: cities

    needling the cracks

☩

The forestmeister will not leave the leaves alone

    bitter cleanliness
    in leafy clandestine
    House of her Flesh
    Let all sleepy leaves
    rest on the forest floor

for the global village of villagers
reaching for high leaves at an angle

†

                    [boom!]—Hope—have it—

†

          The sweet city—what is it? Is that
what you called it?   The one with lights & rubble

where Venus rises over the hills
                and arm-in-arm
                          grackles go

over the silver gutted corpse of burned buildings
    latticed in dust

& people sparkle & speak in big tones of
    small things, speaking
What is "The Good Life"?

      (Now write a 2,000 page thesis)

        (See how the leaf curls   the
                new-green idea of a wintering tree)

When I saw all the little packets
    of human projects from the plane
        & what have you made, there by the river? Let's blow it up —

corrosive clouds of Venus rain down
      —this is how we love each other—

a cascade of voices come from space
or the earthly voice of the angular foot lumbering through stones

Give me boots from the School of
Unified Beauty
to walk with you (you who are studying earth
from inside it)   to interpret
the bend of the knee, tap of the foot, of the living

A creamy froth comes
      tasseling from the top
of corn crops   golden braid
      that the earth sprung forth, kernel by kernel

+

At the mercy of August with not an independent twig to
stake out and sleep on   we were
reduced to sitting around community pools & living rooms
having no thoughts

of the beach-rocks round as dove
eggs and whiter still

That rock makes a
thought, spinning
      out (its word
alters us): a woman sitting in her chair
in Karya, Lefkada, the embroiderer's thread moving

in bright knots   to pattern
the fingers of light
under sea-belly

              trees stitched up beneath
the absolute red heart
of design: a watermelon, a
plum.

What is "The Good Life"?

thought & bone — what — salt — remains of us —

        the beautiful part risen of humans —

"all that can be done flickering aloft
& below" a small flame of life
left   & let gone   let go

BE HONEYED BUSH

Draw the poison
from the Lake with sweet
bait: dip in
sugar sachets & watch
the sirens quake: like
Robot Angels they rise
with eyes of industrial imagination

Sky rolls back to its black
bones & hooks;   We hang.

Could I hear this air tear   to see it
all again — life
with its private   history
moving   particle by particle

Create in us a clean
shirt, clean lake, & of my tongue shall sting

for I have always said
by my true human monster
you too shall be honeyed
in palindromes of gold
when the train divides
your wrong from right

FRAGMENT, UNNUMBERED

the way the architected white
wings unfold in the mind

here I shall attempt to condense
the river, and its music, a lapping
like a can of milk

in this river's sound: superconductivity in vowels
    electrons slide off its fabulous surface

tonight, let's round all the corners
of the house and light the edges

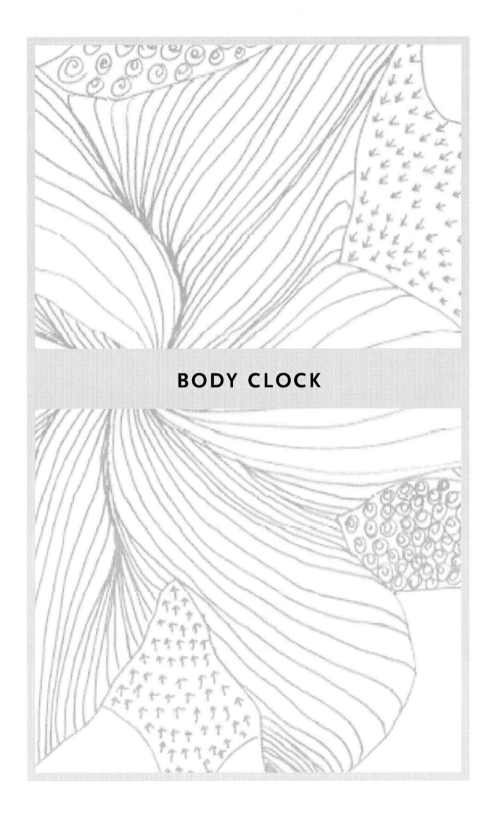

BODY CLOCK

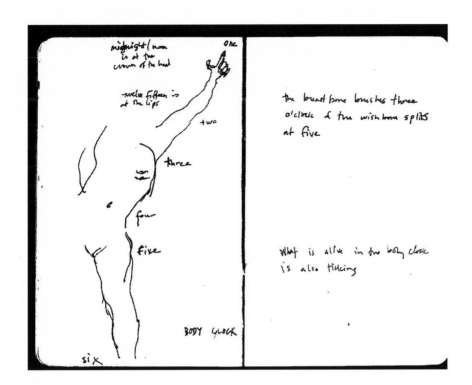

midnight / noon
is at the crown

twelve fifteen is
at the lips

BODY CLOCK

the breastbone brushes three
& the wishbone splits

I wish I were that animal glue
lips animally red

instinct sinewing limb to minute to limb

    the -er you are / I am the bottomer feeder and forager
    the -ing you are / I am and −ed

life takes place in the verb
          a word
transforms into a creature

       in just a grizzled minute
   a *leopard* creeps out of a word

What
will the baby be shaped like?
will she come out round with a red
rose tattoo?

with wing of the ilium?

Body said, *What?*

↓

will she come out innominate
with many parts otherwise unnamed; as, the innominate artery, a great branch of the
arch of the aorta; the innominate vein, a great branch of the superior vena cava

Body said, *What?*

—— bed she built ——

when she lies down   when she arises
from the placenta's vascular sheets

touching all the quantum fields she walked through to
greet me

———————————————————————————————

pools of intricate color collect on the face

———————————————————————————————

There was
the space between [her / his] face and how I felt about it

where sunlight condensed from what once was sun

a perspiration of minutes sweating between us

the door love practiced in me swung open

to look at you and lodge it in my heart

an attitude of love, called Ritual Disaster

Monday, here am I, mortal
machine, clicking in the toothed
metal of time, altricial (born naked and nearly
blind). The traveling bag of my
existence (left lung
slightly smaller to accommo-
date the heart) is having a conversation
with itself (medulla
talking to shin). Your brain too
is having a conversation with the body.
Heart walks down the street, Boston
attached to [a] woman / man / spring day / lovely
in the semilunar valves of the heart
sings

put commas around the baby, put
quote marks around her

have mental custody of
(anything)
the baby

put a text-message-smile on her face

the baby in the body clock

then then then   and
next   this comes
next and   then
put pieces of time next
to pieces of time

in the many directions in which a body grows, it grows
or shrinks in time

put the baby's arms
next to her hands or heart, a

corpuscle a drop of time

a piece of time or blood fell into her heart thus
time began or [time] stopped

What about this
luminous ether, these bumping

atoms, ultraviolet light knocking electrons
off the surface of
a piece of metal?

The numbers and circles with perfect existence
outside the mind?

Gravity's shape on which depends
the flow of time?
_____

Where did the baby come from?

What thing time can't shatter

———————————————

what thing time can time shatter

———————————————

a – z, each vertebrae in the spine, a pony's tail
of nerves bundled at the base singing cat-o'-nine

· · · · · · · ·   ·   · · · · · · · ·

When does time be vertical
when it be horizontally laid
when it be spiky or round

———————————————

a human so shaped like an hour

———————————————

34

If we could shine a flashlight
through the edge of a minute
see the membrane's red
corpuscle, & surface
tension of a second at
the interior atmosphere of an hour
Move the flashlight out
on eternity — possible? Not. (Duh.)

35

In this conception a minute is round though not perfectly — its lines disconnect in the drawing of it to meet up with the next / past minute. You might see the small freckles of scattered seconds at the interior (heart-meat) of the minute.

This is a big-meat minute, true to its actual size, but only took 34 seconds to draw.

This minute took 31 seconds to draw, but accidentally depicts 61 random seconds

I tried a painstaking minute, which took 43 seconds and turned out less beautiful than the quick minute — kind of minute-meat ugly, in fact

What are the parts between the minutes, the seams between, how to count such silent machinery?

Now I will try to draw a

minute that takes exactly a minute. It required me to sometimes speed up, sometimes slow down.

We suddenly began to act
like TV (sitcom) characters, though
we couldn't say why

Someone suggested we had forgotten
how to handle our minutes

Earth shows us how
a minute is round, an hour is, a day

Because it is round we cannot help coming round
upon ourselves again

———————————————————————

Leave room for hope on your list (Hotel Hope)
———————————————————————

As she grows from me to her this
is a field of symmetry

a piece of radish spit into the sink with the toothpaste, its purple shred & white
flesh rattle around the mind, a bit of life

touching all the quantum fields you walked through to
greet me

———————————————————————

Her face is covered with face
———————————————————————

Now the day has a membrane around it slimy and womb-
like that closes at night   with perforations, breathing
holes where the dream rises to the surface;
& opens again in the morning; to begin; to en-
compass all the things we do again   & again   feeding
changing clothing unclothing singing not
singing breathing

meaning has shifted   like jumping color fields on a strip
of button candy   when I say "baby," "the baby," in Colorado's season
of 14 tons of peaches   it means
something new

What thing time can't shatter

_____

watch a yellow
curve, curve yellow — can you? and a
pool of shadow. How the lemon
dives into its own (shadow), or is birthed
from an umbilicus
                    of it like
Venus on a darker wave.
Two pools of shade intersect. You learn
that the lemon has a half-life
of light. This lemon might
hurl itself from space
torpedoing like a sun-field into
the baby-sphere. Yellow [f]lies down in the bed
of the lemon, wakes
the baby who was sleeping there
like a hard bar of sunlight.

a black and white scan of a
troubled young boy's brain
flickers across the screen

interrupted was the conversation
between muscle & tendon, tendon & brain

Little boy's eye, and his brain.
Robin's eye
and crow's

big dog's eye
and little dog's eye.

            Despite the body
the sizes of so many eyes
are almost the same

_____

Fly's eye. And his feet. Tell another story.

_____

A woman steps out of the bath and into a water puddle
on the tile. She doesn't notice Kansas, ocean, surface tension.

The fly steps, and is stuck
in a pool the size of Texas.

What is a second to a hummingbird, a wren
(at heart or wings)? What

is a second to a fly?
"No part of it is negligible"

In the dark we hour it   In the half-light of a veiled world   I minute by minute it
while you collect
& tend to day the hours instead

•   •   •

the baby breathes metonymically

•   •   •

between two hands of the clock
    the world assembles

second hand sings out:
    and and and

"I would out-night you"

Skim through the penumbra (pale
outer fringes), the moon-spill will, of Earth's shadow

——————————————

Night, a mind's natural shift
——————————————

at the bottom of this dark Western Night Road

Time rolls by invisible until it hits

glass-bottomed world, feet
scuffle over the dead

——————————————

There was the boy for whom everything had to occur in its opposite motion.

Time was at issue

gnawing at the minute's edge, glowing cartilage
& bone of a minute; Shave off
a snack of time, a crunchy
minute, jellied minute, an overripe
mushy minute

(A minute pinks the seeds of thought)

(a corpuscle a drop of time)

the sensorium (Body Hotel) being the story of
how we fell from timelessness to time

In May, the limbs were still jerky, unfreezing
at the joints, ligaments
in arabesque

By June, we move in
perfect symmetry

You're in the minute, and it's not
history, then you're on the other side, and
it is. What happened to
what happened there?

If we increase the surface
of a minute, give it
absorbtive properties

A shaggy minute, hairy minute, lop-
sided
minute exploding at its edges like an
oily egg all ooze, a
minute wheeling away

it broke open & cut
my lip — did — discover — what
the inside
of the body-minute (meat-minute)
tastes like

TOWNSHIP
OF CAUSE OF TROUBLE

A RADIANT COUNTESS OF WHAT'S IT

I love it
when women eat sweet ribbon, sweet
rabbit, sweet meat, when women

are the scene
of several utopias

when the body melts back into shadow
beginning with the feet

Begin
tonight. When does the synecdoche appear? When the mall,
the garden? What parallel shapes
in the mind made of
traps and steel? Violence at the edges
of experience. When, "my clan forbids it"? The silent b
of *bombing*?

As suggested by the top of the whorled shell
Dandelions made a milky ring
A spiral galaxy at which point touched
the world wide web
A wet nose print where the dog sniffed stone
A puppet laid down in its little dirt bed
Bridges were constructed of aerial systems
A man crouched in a field recording crickets
Among dandelions without their feathered caps sat four ladies, hatless

The soldier tied himself to a tree, a branch
broke, it was
juniper, the humblest
bush to which a man's hand holds
Bodies once lay here, moistened by spit and dried by time
See where a hip grazed the ground
map of a place we once found, grid
of high tension
leaves
a robin
warped its singing
to match all streams

A mouth totally emptied out
the world's sound
                    and the wind
crashing in
to a mouth   whistles out
a world akin

to the house finch's song:
It it it   hey it   hey it

NOTES TOWARD THE TOWNSHIP
OF CAUSE OF TROUBLE
(VENUS'S CABINET REVEALED)

Here we are wandering in the world of things

to find a happiness seed
unfolding in a corner
of the house

like a minute sloughing off
its seconds and parts

find magic in a hopeless crystal

a house poem in the house

videlicet: that is, namely
videre: to see
licet: it is permitted

[reader must dream
a few nights' dreams here
before continuing]

a dream beneath the city made bones rise up
and made the struts for churches

and told us

study: graveyards, gravesites
study: mirrors

a town's mirror is dug underground
a tooth's in its roots
the living in the dead

a ripple near a lamb's eye
(approximates)
the curves of a cloud
the eye itself a bullet

this feather or fur keeps returning through the eye or the ear as its word

the sun, for example, a central fact
around which the head spins, heats up the mind

a city might be drawn lightly
with a pencil and left that
way, as if
all we needed to live in was a sketch

to ostensify, ossify   a house, its language, body

a word gathering there goes brittle

what is the meaning of this? *it*
unfolds, refolds
over time

The planispheres of the heavens
are systematically represented
but it is disputed how
much practical knowledge
is embodied there

to pour my heart down on
(Niger yellowcake)

to find the plant of birth
(war record on human hide)

We inhabit rooms never touched by death
(a separate house for that)

"to be eating dandelions from the root"
(*manger les pissenlits par la racine*)

a parsley seed travels to Hades three times
(before it sprouts)

Utah, Nevada, Arizona's grasses flushed with rads

hemoglobin bubbles & nebulas wobble
a *vol nuptial*, bridal flight of blood & bees

(to no longer be worried for)
(what one doesn't know)

(to no longer feel)
(responsible for it)

the body, often at odds
with us, tense
in its own disbelief of itself

a fly flying in
to meet its shadow on the ceiling

the letter is transient, the hand
is permanent, spell the vowels
in a palm

Tonight all the festivities
under the earth will cease
Tonight all the celebrations
will be above ground

What is this pile of
darkness in the room?

a silver-coated plate
bathed in iodine vapor
will
capture your face, a hummingbird
caught in a cage

a palace made
of a million pounds of plate glass
will now
collapse

the study of hands in the light, of touch
in the dark

a child having always the Book
of her hands open before her eyes

some radiant history

some restless meat I feel

some empathy for the hard-line military man who died
& saw the error

the shoes that are too
tight to walk in my hand

change the self-pitying war narrative
to Bag of Trees
Upfull & Bright

seen from air : a
telephone pole's most
charming shadow

what was the tree

the land : one big raggedy   ghostly sonnet

the heart beats in each pore
of the body like a red
pinprick

you were dragging something
from the black interior out

how one man can make
the march of history
bear down on you, what turns on the edge
of a blade

the afternoon light glowing through her teeth as she talked

what the will will do
is not always what the heart would
perhaps rarely what the mind

now go learn some animal things

the fold at the juncture
of butt & thigh where the sun
didn't reach

she shows it to us

how a sentence or a line
cannot reverse time

it turns out we were made
from piles of shit she asks

red as red blood pooling on the thumb those geraniums
in window boxes on this street

bed of earth, bed
of air why not
a bed of fire too

double le temps, et
puis le vendre

clods & clouds
mercify me

a landscape might melt
back up toward a city

like this erotic site of decay
(the body)

from the cunt to the head is
a Möbius strip
that connects us to death

& some scissors trim all time as does
the eye or mind

No more fooling around
Make a thing of such
extreme beauty it cracks
and cracks
the hand that makes it

The hour which once was square
rubbed at its clitoral
corners turns round

pieces of a second shaved off (like metal filings)

the frictioned minutes (castaways) lie in wait for
that true magnet time[i]

How reversible?: "knowledge is contained / in
the world / being in /
self"

Head: let the skull bones slide apart
& the brain grow big

type: orb
shape: universal

stepping on the rind of earth
below which that trash heap Hell

It seemed impossible to tell
what country we lived in

some sad gray faces pass

a brown dwarf, a
          failed star

in the blended light of a planet & its sun
the dust & the photons rise

          Butter Princess, I saw
a huge cross of lights laid out in the land
& it was some city
between Sioux Falls & Detroit

i   when & where the labyrinthodont am-
phibians lived, & I quietly loved
you in opposite fashion   like
certain small crystals making topaz yolks in the balking veins
of the earth   swimming
toward what will soon become rock, the needle
        shivering in the dark
toward a new magnet   a heart
of a world even travels
toward other poles
North South North South

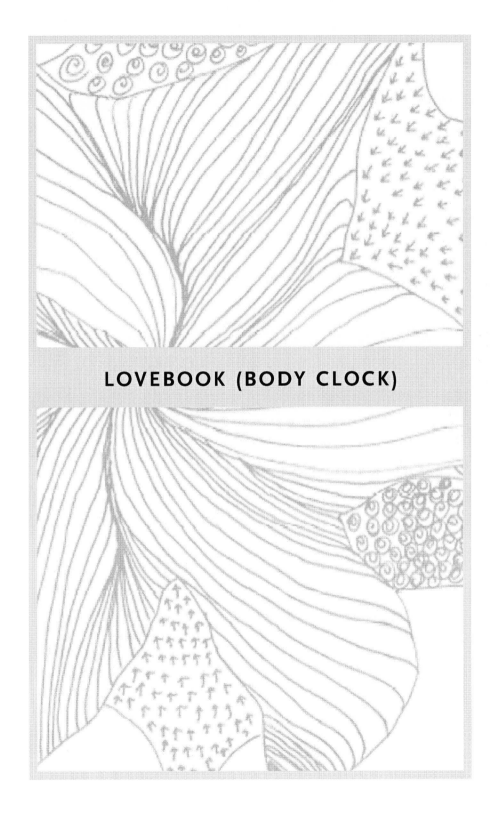

LOVEBOOK (BODY CLOCK)

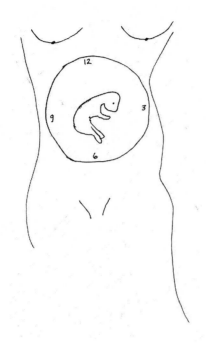

to which hour does she grow
to which   attach
how these hours stick to her
dark the window

heeyá! in the night   who gladdens stars as
if horses
and holding the reins holding
little wolf-wigs to a bird, stars in in centrifugal spin, heeyá,
do-ggy, unsweet little
turd in your paper pants on the plane that I must
change & I must change my mind about you daily as we
revolve around the sun you say
apple up mama baby hola kitty bye-bye hi papa hello
you poke your head out & inventory: *WA A A A!* busiest
self-propelled motorist / tourist / windmill removing
all the adulterated items from my purse and
breaking all the adulterated items in my
purse and we love it, biter, you, your
hectic hands and all that traffic you produce which has to do
with meteors and books and brains and words and poop
and constellations made the stars you make of humans

Straight from my Robot Womb
comes this grandiloquent news
to be shouted on sidewalks
        and on freeways, straight
from my robot womb

a pebble hurries toward its destination, rattling
like Homer's Greek in the dark

into the smooth moraine that was
the baby's mouth, ouch, a jagged cloud razors
the gums, raggedy, like a mad signet, sure
sign and seal

of the human: more body, more tooth, more
apple, more thought

the back of her bald head is
innocent, traveling in total darkness
through the moon's night, shadows, ice

what cluster of thought (genes) made a voice
that could crack a drop of turquoise
stone, a tear, the shape of truth

a granite tooth, a patch of white and brittle time

(cosmographikos universalis)

       hung in the dream as mirrors of a day
a day's
       domestic things: blue
        -rimmed dish,   ribboned
                      baby's shoe   , Shine
              things, more beautifully in the dream's dark
oilcloth, backdrop against which all objects of the day might parade
       hypothetical & new like if we re-made an alphabet
       from scratch, from yellow rain slickers sliced up & used
              as A's and E's — vowels so
       radiant they're waterproof

the best nude thing
    best naked thing
                 a baby

night naked night
night common night
                baby night

your night is sometimes stained with love

little piglet! We survived
the longest night of the year, its dawn brown
hand waving through the window
my undiscursive daughter, you
pressed against me rooting Siree! You were born
& now you've torn our nights
to shreds & watch the minutes tumble inconsequential but
of consequent is every second
your supersize ears grow
away from you bumping Now
buckle down to baby-like which is your job since you've
severed from the Babyerium   a bead a bead in the long
string of living
things how
the Ferris wheel of Barcelona will show you more world

dropping the baby,
hurting the baby, the baby
hurting, dying   dying the baby
leaving the baby in a tub of
bombs   water the baby falling into a pool
shrapnel   the baby
nails bundled together   the baby
bombs and blown   the baby
H. and
A.
bombs
thermonuclear morning   the baby
desert with no color   the baby
over which a sun white sun   the baby
there is no color left that
rises
no plant
to be frosted
no lizard
to be burned

mother, baby, world, everybody's getting whipped

Time might wrap around you in a darkened room
beneath a felted cloak feel a felted arm
the sweet-gadget gets carried   by my hips   I've forgotten
to take my vitamins / take out the trash I was caught
in a slow tail of time, feet like a fly's
in a water puddle, sometimes we feel the hour in which
hydrogen sticks
to oxygen, hear
its suction and situation, know
surface tension at the top
of the minute's bubble   This is not the comet's tail of time but
a crystalline airdrop in the corner of the eye like
          a reverse tear   when the face is underwater
                    you might see a tear of air   when
      would such a tear be shed

"To float the ear in beauty"
to singe an eyelash on truth
ruth to
burn the eye (world)
tweak the elbow on love to
scintillate the armpit with
whose liver to bonk your knee on righteousness
to rub lakes out
smack the nose on space
to wear a pollen gown
shout out the sea's sound-shadow
a baby wrapped in an orange hour
hiding there

we did not know which hour blanketed the baby   was it
Shark's egg   or rose?

          what violas are you
            hiding in your mouth, little
night-time cave half-rocked
about, a dim purpling
of words shouts there
to get out

_____

a batmobile revs

_____

I do see language in the trees it's
known as "leaves"

      • • • • • • •

hwuff hwuff hwuff

About Being Dead

_____

You wouldn't know, biscuit-hand
you're so alive

_____

Cherry Tree
(The Rape)

each word opened upon
the limb, kissed the skin teeth-tiny

•

a blossom unfolded its serrated kiss

•

the sting of the flower, not
the bee

•

the blossom misplaced its minute, I mean its *tiny* smog-dusted microscope

•

Fragment, unnumbered

                 a book

of hours made of body
fluids   the skull falls
       into ruin, rain .

   now warm the winter throat
of my loves

79

tulip, tell us
      how   to go moving
              (daylight, wind)
heart, I don't own it   not its
   work

              poinging away

Porous her name was   was her face
her always changing face   Worrow Joyrous
heart-dirt poured down on it

WORLD IS WEIRD

WORLD IS WEIRD

World is weird, and so
what? Water this poem and watch it
take shape, it's layers
of the born
world, heard
world, streaked and shaved, see
it shakes, a
shuttle carrying
all world's weeds, weirds,
trash and goods, gods to you —

Or perhaps it's winter's ordinary scene:
abandoned tires in marsh-shore muck
The highway goes by it, and ducks take
to airways about now

Water World is on the right
Next left No-Oxygen World, Dry World, Dirt World, Tin
World and World of Exemplary Vehicular Noises

Exit the poem for: Sluice City, World of Steel, Plug-In City with Maximum
Pressure, an
                Asphalt-and-Weed Oasis

Find here: Vacant sky, vacant lots, a few
                    Sunday faces nuclear cascading

Of the world, weird: People wear it, "the section they use
like clothes on their backs," and soon appears "an object as
magic as a private face"

PLECTRUM

my winter finger, spring finger
    plucked a corrosive-wove thing from earth
& let it drop till music appeared,   a
    hand-carved delirium net to let
         what in
dactyls are demons   the ivory gate
       is the hand and   also the mouth
to shatter day's poison
shutter the hand and   and also the mouth
  Night,   we x-
      cloister the papers   corrode them
      as if song were an acid
Here is the day's good news

ACHILLES ON A BALL *(Leather Leaping Toward Light)*

There's a house stuck to my arm, it's
      red, a barn. Language sticks
      to the corners of the house & sands smooth
      rough spots
      of the self.
                      Just so

Achilles steps & steps but
    can't seem to escape the
    roundness of the shield

      a tiger on a ball, the
world   the
face may hold
onto the skin years
and years   bone   leaping through

like a pair of ivory honey-scissors
          slitting leather
               and leather
     leaping toward light

Bones escape their sack, veil themselves in dirt

    Stains on the page are
      of the body or are
        bones evading their bag

Will it be one of these bones
or backyard faces, black,
     to be hammered in gold?

The body's stain returns to the body, a
  backward pleasure
  like dusted wings that refold
  a lucky wounded symmetry or
  the lips of the cunt closing

(This lily pad stem fits there.)

From the flat field of war (wound), Achilles tumbles out

Flat because it happens
at this point in time & in that
at this point on earth & on that

The body exposed like stone
to wind or word, erodes

METAMORPHOSIS:
BABY WITH A SQUARE HEAD (TRAIN RIDE)

They're making food for us
out in the fields. In little
patches of muddy earth, in
tufted lumps of brown and grown green
men are digging with hands or machines and
they're growing stuff
ready
for us to eat.

the flooded cornfield is full of vision

They probably already said "the lakes like
turquoise teardrops," rain's
big cry-baby eyes.
                              The train

that hunts a place haunts the eye, speeding by
in the other direction, other dream.   They
have said or seen
stranger things
than lorries loaded with pipeline,

89

the sky made deadly with shrapnel, *l'invention de la vie*, living
phrases left unfinished

> The square of death grows
> like an overfed baby, big
> baby with a square head

bits and kinds of life
left over, lying there:
a stub of bird, nothing fancy, a little sparrow or crummy starling
crusty husk of some pill-bug gone brittle
an egg, its
        thoughtful arrow inside

sea urchins like miniature sea machines rustling their levers, they
bristly, brightly, smile

J-curve of the polar
bear's yellowed heels as it hikes
across the ice

> Puncture this list.

> We will use them all, these
> smudges of life, all
> bibelots belong to us

DAY — NIGHT / HERE — OUT
(THIS INDUSTRIAL ROOM OR DAY)

A soft fleece wigs the aspen.
A velveteen shade lovingly staffs the grasses.
Clouds do dark work upon rocks.
Hussy buds   totally naked   flirt & fidget on plums.

                                              Huddled are dumb

houses licked by sidewalks   If I stepped
off and across, I would bump
into physics   I guess   I have
no idea who lives here   The ante meridiem sun

is thugging
it up over the tiny seed-sized inhabitants.   Hands become handsome

boats in this talkative
city of ropes where the sun
tunnels and pockets emblems
of whatever river exists here.   They call this
precipitation.
                      Bones go
concrete, under duress.   I'd like to
        pirate myself out   perform surgery
        on a town —   lift off the roofs, stitch them back, rearranging
        streets, arteries, veins   What is the weather

            in Baghdad?   Glass, rocks, & twigs

            fall from trees.
                            Now the palest
      legs of the most

earthly woman ever
to wear socks have
just sliced past the unforeseen and deepest green
juniper   Listen: sparrows

sweetly racketeering, crashing
into trees, wingy des-
peradoes throw feather-&-bone
blows.   A spiderweb threads

through sunlight. You can hear the wheels before you see them: small
bike tires kissing each brick.   Thunderous
noise of Human Walking: keys clank   feet creak, etc. and then
thought working quietly inside the house of the skull, coordinating muscle which
engages bone, then worrying about [roadside bombs, coffee] etc.

        (The FBI agent steps out of the room, takes a call.)

        A leaf scuds across concrete, its
        brittle sails coughing.

        This big square where we find ourselves

is flat & boxed
then humped & ragged
to the north; there are huge mountains rising
up that give way to

dust & sand. There are soldiers hiding
under a hill with secret signals, a red button and
weapons.   To the south, the after-hours
ghosts haunt the
Wal-Mart
aisles.   In evening's hedging light surely

there is a valley and there are grasses, a lot
of democrats, republicans   I don't know how to think of it
without mentioning the Mississippi   the malfeasant
president   which adjusts the shapes of this
place & wings us
accordingly   The state

line wavers under the
pressure of thought &
hardens under politics, squiggly
ghost child gone
colorful and bad

      And so *stare decisis* enters our common
   tongue   around the bones of history   language
                grows brittle with
  objects & thoughts   Let the flesh
    loosen, fall

       off   & I will awake in a coffin-sized
               shell, outer
               body gone mute
               inner life rioting like a murder of crows

What rolls toward sleep
in nyctitropic precision
as we ourselves roll toward the dark
& the leaves & the plants
take up new positions
for midnight — How might
this mirror the shapes a

sky or constellation makes
as it winks in the mind
of a beholder? Workers tracking
the days on Mars are losing
sleep. On this wall are switches
that determine how light or how
dark is our night — all our tropic
bodies move toward the light.   We'll make a bed

in this city on which our helixes
will rise and bend and I will not want

to change this day
& its sad contained it's still its
I mean, there is rain.

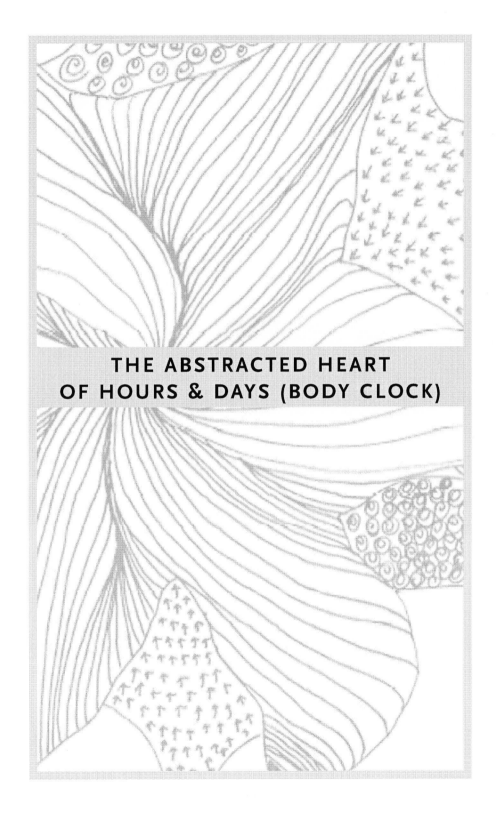

THE ABSTRACTED HEART
OF HOURS & DAYS (BODY CLOCK)

an hour is not an hour
if it takes 1 minute
48 seconds to draw

A / The day is made up of air — light & —
Air —   How can we look
Through the window and say
We see it there?

First experiment with an hour

I

I (FIRST HOUR'S RESIDUE)

12:50:09 p.m. the hour begins

when I see a button at the middle of the hour (flower) holding the hour's fabric/folds in place

how I see I drew a flower to rhyme with hour in sound and shape

and at its eye the empty center   a wind sockles the hour's clothesless intentions

because I am told the hour is directional THE EYE BECOMES ENTANGLED IN AN ARROW

I had thought to make a marker, indicate

the first line to fit the structure   of   an hour but that hour's arrow was overtaken   by other
arrows

one misstep   will ruin this hour

99

1:24:50 pm now I have filled the hour's outer petals with arrows the baby
cries she is hun
gry

I do not suffer
symmetrophobia
I see symmetry and asymmetry
unfold   that is
just like an
hour   its amours   arrows as
gleeful spermatozoa
rushing to me

I see this corner (petal) of the hour peaking   like an ancient
wave, a shark's fin or an
antique prow   inside are
capsized e's
             curled needles, gleaming golden sharp

three scales on the minutes like those
on the round-scaled spearfish whose
tail is bright   glowing blue   I wrote "minute," meant minutes inside an "hour," blue

my inside minutes are getting slop-happy   divers gasp for air

I think seconds are peeling off the hour   are petals   floating into a vast   distance   overhead
the floorboards creak, the humans I
love and live with   there seem to be
spikes at the edges of my hour like a
gold-tipped fence   who could climb an hour's fence? who, fall into the hole
1:50:48

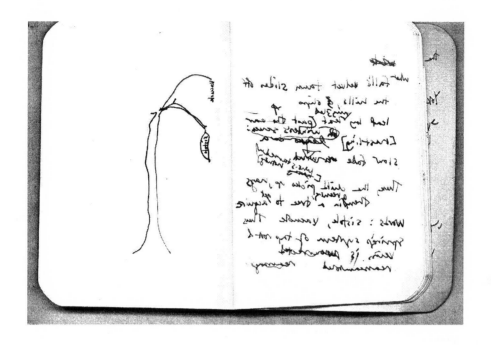

fall's velvets slide off the hill, slip,
leaf, past the ear   nuzzle
winter's screen. Slow fade. These (leaves)
the child (who started with nothing)
picks up, hangs in a tree, greening, to get
"sistole," "vacuole"   thus is spring's system of taproot and veins
reassembled article by article, seam by seam

summer doesn't stop weaving
threads around her and will wind up felting us in a warm velour of years

like in some parks a statue is wrapped
in the emerald fur of trees

an hour hides itself inside the body, burrowing for later misuse
(how many disguises we wear with just our own flesh)

an hour rolls forward across the floor
till we are rib-old thinking time prevents

(bathed in what color of years)

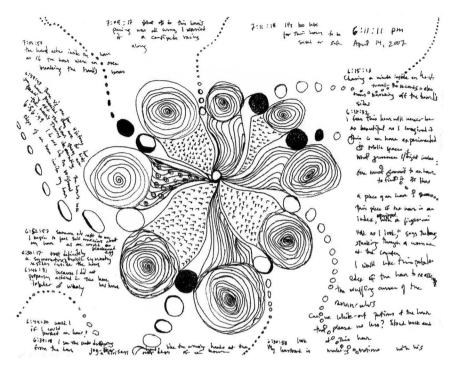

Second experiment with an hour

2

---

² (Second Hour's Residue) (public)

Chasing a minute inside an hour's burrow — the second-elec

     trons knocking off the burrow's

  sides

...

a piece of an hour I mean

this piece of its index is

equipped

with ratios, reasons

"old as I look," says the hour,

speaking through a woman at the counter

I would like this petal-edge of the hour to reassemble a ranunculus, to

white out portions of the hour that please us less   Stand back and

look   at this hour   its hands waving at the out out edges

• • •

would I if I could perfect an hour?   I see the seeds dripping
from this hour   "jog-bear," a girl says

• • •

because I did not properly attend   to it this hour has turned
tubular & wooly

• • •

someone sits next to me   I begin to feel self-conscious about my hour as one would a blackened
egg

• • •

These v's are for victory   how
an hour prevailed   They are for birds   peeling off the hour's surface   They are
the hour's thorns decorating the hour's rose

• • •

the hand aches inside the hour
as if the hour were an oven
      breaking the hand's bones

We've graduated to hours.
And the folds between minutes.
The crumpled folds between hours.
They keep adding dimensions to space not time. Why? The folds
the felt folds why the folds between minutes and hours.

You may wish to mention the old boogers in the bathtub. (No thanks.)

The night line descends
  carcajou you
              wolverine
                    of night

an hour an iron collar relaxing
   into the undone
              threads   night nights itself

a morning, an hour arrives   tense as streetlights reflected in rain gutters

an hour shines like a wound
the debris of hours accumulated in the face   an hour
like a wrecking ball   an hour
in mid demolition   a pirouette, performance, an
hour smashing, wounding   the face

You speak only of an hour's destruction.

Here, spicules were built. Assembled
into a needle-like house. Transparent. Airy. Gorgeous. Constructed
to withstand all time.

What? says Body.

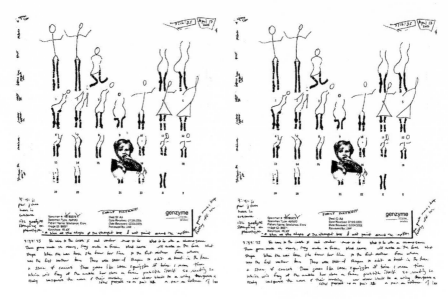

Third experiment with an hour

3

---

3 (THIRD HOUR'S RESIDUE)

3:44:45 We come to the dark double x and wonder   what does a chromosome worry

whose genes carry ovary   make a face   what name   arrive on the face   what

shape   When born she drew a line   to the first mother   from whom

was the first mother burned   There were several shapes to edit   a knot in the knee

a string of cancer   these genes like loose squiggles of time   I mean twine

which will fray at the ankle (time)   go dust at the calf   the hour does a face

Unsquare the hour of its making   her elbow bleeds to a wing   a sibyl

          propped on 22 pairs of evidence

part of an hour is erasure   like genotype stomping on phenotype

     a blur at the edges of the thought box & wet paint around the caption

her macroscopically visible aspects (46,xx)   in her haploid cell she sneezes to show she's

     (the quote marks keep falling off her)

ghosted   the teeth of   radiance

                                        /petals   /letters like

the hour takes tweezers

to its hairs   4:46:35

what derives of the Desiring heart

---

cries [/] unfurl in the

                        night

            & unfold me

A snake is holding the world in its jaws, the world is suspended there. Nothing touched the tooth, lips, lids, mandibles. Nothing touched the hour, nothing touched the world.

The poem can be as risky as the body. Male & Black, Female & White. The body lies quivering with self and self-doubt. The body covered with question marks. (Each pore punctuated by it.) Lick it all over with your mirrored tongue. I mean there is another body in the bed. This adds and subtracts doubt.

I saw the nursing mouth occlude the nipple, and the person collecting there, under the eye's delicate glass dome of the eyes. (Identity travels
with the milk.)

I had thought the person disperses in pleasure but hour by hour the baby assembled herself there.

---

a. the mamma & the
   pappa lie down

b. the baby sends sound
   waves far

c. a minute expands into
   an hour

she   calls   I

answer   swer   a swerve   a
brush of air   I swear   a scarf
        a scarving her answer
    answer me

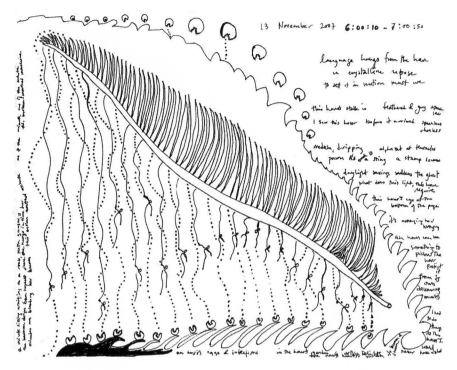

Fourth experiment with an hour

4

---

4 (FOURTH HOUR'S RESIDUE)

       language hangs from the hour

               in crystalline repose

     to set it in motion   must we

The hour's stalk is feathered & gay

I saw it before it arrived shoeless helpless speechless

medusa dripping poison A's   each B a sting a stamp because because

daylight savings saddens the ghost

it's amazing how hungry an hour can be   Hand me something
to pillow the hour, protect it from its own devouring minutes

I had to do things to this hour I would never have wished

In the hour's-heart's garden of earthly delights

A minute sat with gnashing teeth waiting on a rock

The human drips from herself where she hangs in time her minutes are bleeding   her bream   a
broken-mouthed minute

as if the minute   as if the minute   broken-mouthed machine

of all the world's
  marsh gas
  tear gas
      (lacrymogenic) made
  to make me cry

---

    shattered across the bed: baby,
      bodies

    gods above   their counterparts
    below   scattered
    across a mirror of time

---

      the tear is locked in a wingcase

              elytron

     let loose again later

   lampyridae   a glowworm a firefly

tear become

    my Variable Intensity Rain Gradient Aloft
    nimbostratus virga over the desert or a day

---

    there's a microburst when light particles drift

    & clouds and tears dressed up as ice crystals melt
    before they hit the ground

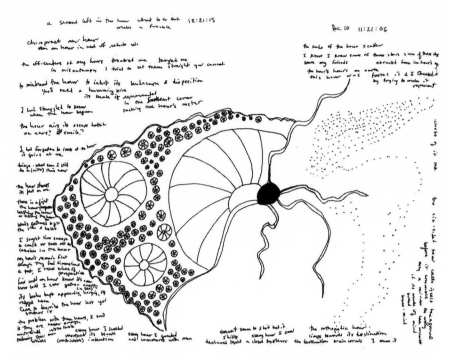

Fifth experiment with an hour

5

---

5 (FIFTH HOUR'S RESIDUE)

11:21:06

the hour's seeds scatter
I know I knew some of these stars   some of these stars
were friends
                    abstracted
from the hour's ego   the hour's hours   on earth

Clouds fall   the six-sided hour calls itself   hexagonal

                                        orthopedic   the hour
limps   toward its destination   the destination brain corals   I mean it
doesn't seem to but it   shifts
                                    every hour I saw declared itself a closed system
every hour I greeted   had commerce with men   every hour I scolded mouthed its blank
(unprintable) intention
every hour geoded   into something weird and good

the problem with these hours, I said

is they are   untrained intractable   following their own whims

how could I ever gather enough (marry hour to hour)?

Unwed, its holes kept tearing, hungry, its   rough-rag hem

Cease to describe the hour lest you smother it

Mother   my hours though feeling dimensional go flat   I lack   tricks of perspective

I sought time enough to caulk all the crevices in an hour
words gather to fill the holes

        lashing the hour   or letting the hour be
the hour stomps   its feet on me   (triage)

I had struggled to know   when the hour began   to mind-read the hour   to intuit its
                                                landscape & disposition
        you'd need a hummingbird
                sucking the hour's nectar
        (its beak represents   through the southeast corner)

the off-centers of my hour   tangled me
        in anthropy & misanthropy   I tried to set them straight you cannot
        chiropract an hour   even an hour in need

12:21:15

This house is a little haunted, it's
my body   body-house

    bones rising to the surface in the night   sinking
back before daylight

what parent pain we carry
several more than 40 years

the way a crumpled can will flash
from the roadside in certain angles of light
like a flashing eye or

what derives of the desiring heart, blinking in the dark

I guess I'd say plurality bleeds in

I emptied the body satchel out. Of course it was a womb. Cat's claws, whiskers,
hair-nuts, snarl husks, everything
that collected in the sheets ground to a fine
powder nearly erased
by history (a day's work). We named her
Eva Grace.

She knits herself an everything head

  makes herself into a
       scary animal

    a scarred star or

some blank thing from
                    far
                        afar

this was a girl trying all the things
    to get from baby to big

The live cat claws the night
for sounds like
sharpened rain

WEEK-IN-REVIEW

for / from Paul Fattaruso

Someone shot a million billion neutrinos through Minnesota and found one or two at the other end.

Lake Superior was the starting place.

Zacarias Moussoui who did not participate in the 9/11 bombings will not be sentenced to death.

My body speaks the same language as walls, all our electrons charged.

A charismatic storm rolls in and lays the buds flat.

The baby could not be stopped, waved and ate a crab apple blossom.

Night day night day a Maytag
cycle & sun an amniotic rock like a golden loogie in the sky.

An atom for whom it is hard to interact with matter.

I cannot see event but a white ghost glinting, rolling
            over the horizon.

But mothering makes us ambidextrous.

Objected by a house.

Clear the dishes out.

Please find my shoes, flax blue. Something's winking in the yard.

A peak upon which the sun never sets.

Dreamt these symbols: "I [   ] my red
river valley,   my red
coat, red dress.   :   will always
have ; had   ;
have had ;   will always have had"

The dream-having shifts as if
what we could do or be in tiny gradations and import is
constantly escaping.

A river transforming into a boat
& you, the rider.

And dreamt a whip that tortures itself.

To settle in dark mantle deposits, the moon's maria
To land in the Lake of Excellence
(A slow boat for cargo, fast taxi for humans)
To leap in itinerant air

What is a "wave of violence"?
What is the Delta Force? Who
blew up the bridge? Who jumped in the lake?

(After laughter slaughter of
   the low
            roses.)

The man with black leather wristbands and a double chin

leads us to the next transformation
and I ask, but how much is spectacle & how much is real? How much
is spectacle, how
much real?
Spectacle & Real, Spectacle & Real (I am
looking into his face).[1]

Whosoever has almost drowned will never
trust water again.

Not a *glass* of water?
Not a glass of *water.*

I think it depends on what kind of person you are — do you
find the limits & then
start kicking?

The will collects with the world.
Or
The will collects against it.
It collects with it as we grow
   into or toward the world
         & then it collects against it.

What do you mean by that?

How a river rhymes with
small variations in the structure

Sea's strophes, a push
and receding of sound — hush
and roar — hush
and roar

language loving each
rock (syllable) as it comes in
then pushing it off

what shatters the sky

a fact's decay in time

rolling around

I didn't know what to say that I hadn't already said so I stopped
talking about it (political / world situation)

like the sound shadows of the ocean

a word creeps out of her mouth, appears
in the curve (lip & tongue)

it's not missing its b's but its final consolation

boo(k)   boo(b)   bir(d)   bom(b)ing

Is that sea surrounded by land or land
surrounded by sea?

(*The body exposed like stone
to wind or words, erodes*)

Internally displaced
earthquake-watching stars

Nick Ranger, arms dealer, doesn't know
if his guns have fallen
into the hands of rebels, i.e.,
Fuck you

A wave makes a slapping sound
at the happy meeting of land and water, and the slap
is carried through air

Where did I begin with a light in
the mouth carried
from somewhere
else

Continent's light and dark scurries
through night, south

Dreamt I had to kill a man
in order to stop the
cramps in my legs & hand

I was in Abu Ghraib and Laird
was my friendly jailer

I succumbed to the snowy
ornithology of the North
the bittern histology of the East

when we become that creature that I am[2]

Let me slip off the front
brain
or any brain
Let me slip off my brain
so useless / in the face
of face /
how to not be face but be

daylight's order decays me midmorning

nighttime's world of close chaos comes in

as birds might say I've lost my compass

Can you give me prices
on baby legs and a
high hat?

Carelessly

a small chunk of her arm was carried off by a wasp, hair
by the form of hills.
What pleases me here? Hair, her
hair her hills

That is, my savannah has crawled over to dust.

Shrapnel huddled in the mud, smiles brightly
at a glint of sun

a clock that keeps moving then telling
time

The president was unsure which to advise: chrystotherapy or chrysotherapy?
        christ or gold   christ or gold

evening bursts through the doors
who holds the sky back

a turn signal winks flirtatious

a body lobs a ball, a ball
lugs itself through air

a body looks forward
to what evolution can restore

of mammals animals Cenozoic their storehouse source (the body, sun)

far from stars they structure
and repeat themselves concrete

(humans)

found an ancient forgotten riverbed named "Realealea"

is more real, as a dream is more real
than the president

---

[1] pigeons fall
from the building, delicate & full
of grace like swoops
of white waves collapsing in
silence or
falling snow, in suicide-
leaps; pearling gray
leaves
that fly back
up again
to their trees—

[2] Creation is violet I thought reality
blue, but it was just my
thinking, which is
yellow and
everything that touches touches you
turns to something
you can hear being its
brown and pink, twingeing
scratching

CONTENANT ET CONTENU
(This was on a bottle of shampoo.)

The water evaporates from the glass,
the child outgrows her shoes, the wood
erodes, the paint chips, the painting fades,
the leg breaks, the war
explodes.

What is the body's container?
From soldiers we learn about each other.
Nothing is contained.

---

unstoried soul a stoned dark doll a
soul doesn't tell stories
it's a baby playing in
the poles of the universe   — did you mean puke?
War is how we know each other.

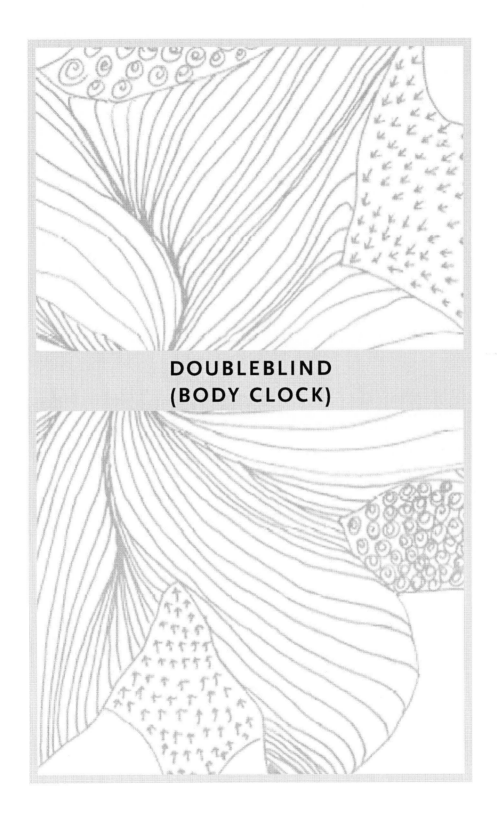

DOUBLEBLIND
(BODY CLOCK)

why is midnight the hollow crux,
   resting on a V — apex, ilex

why I saw it sickness unfolding
   empty as an egg (*cascarone*)

 a volcano pointing down
    & up — midnight points too

back through the hours of the night &
   forward to the hours of the day

  Midnight is a cunt that way

Sleep so edge-yellow it browns violet's belly, black-eyed

                                         hungry,   sandy at the margins

You break glassy sleep, shattering the lid

           Spread on a hillside

I lay on the ground with sleep, panting.

Sleep was hovering, gummy, jerry-rigged above

our downy bed.   It dropped and bounced, rubbery

& transitive.

What conversation sleep had

with the dream, what contraband and argument!

Sleep's yellow does not leap who says I say

sleep pounces or sleep delays

               stubborn as a rubber

duck in a slip of sunlight.   Sleep spread a

sudden domestic golden aura running

my night's shroud. Sleep withered, it shrunk, it

does not want to touch me. Sleep tugged

at the body, too heavy, too spidery

& webbed, lugged it across the night like a tarantula   Resplendent night responded:

too *heavy*, human! so heavy. and light.

The body was an eyelash skittering

across the hours, bumping over midnight

& sleep a grainy ghost,

a spirit that hovers close to the fogged mouth, the mist on a river, a mirror a baby

breathes out

It's all to eat the eye

in sleep's double-blind
                    Sleep
devours the eyes / from the inside

how deep does the eye look in in
sleep

        or through years, self's

eating centuries there

Did any hundred years lie down and did we
Lie down quietly in sunlight   Did
Any century leap windbreaks in silence
Like a lunged dog-devil
Did any century not crush
Not crash not gnash and creak
Not gnarl did any century
Not devour not mountain not
Man not amused nor woman nor river nor child
thicket nor arm
No century was ever an asylum
It was never a valley never
        A long deep sleep

What did we do for rest then?
Why did we ever say "fullness" for wake?
Sleep is less empty. Something is sullen.
Sleepfulness.
In one atomic instant sleep
waked over sleep
worked over it was
the water of waking, walking
the air of sleep. Sleep
was not the underside of the chin's coin, not day's eroding spine on
dark's discus, sleep
did hover below the horizon, pillowed
in a cloud — what kind of cloud? Not a sleep
cloud, mushroom cloud deflating, something like light muffled by

                                                     eyes & their lids.

Sleep, span tendon & thistle, golden, nor gossamer, fleshly and

                                                    breakable.

Whatsoever a fingertip severed whatsoever
entered the ear
Was that about waking?
a book you could read, of Wake and of Sleep, with pictures
of fabulously sleeping beasts. In heaven or in sleep safe
in my zone of non-knowledge. My inside animal lost & most
precious (to me). The baby did not wake, she did not cry,
she did not move toward the windows, not toward the light. And waking
replied, What was the sleeper's role, what
the worker's? She was only a ghost
making sleep and not-sleep
to slip through a woke.

the dreams are mirrors of the day
the days are mirrors of the dream

a tall black man is walking in the shoulder of the road, night,
which is where I'm walking too. He says softly, What's your
name. Turn my head softly, what's yours? Frangipans, he says.

• • •

in sleep I learn a black man may cast a white shadow
just as a white woman might throw a black one
whether or not they know it
on either side of the outside body, dance

• • •

"with reflections in mirrors, with shadows, with guardian spirits, with the belief in the soul and with the fear of death"

double the snow leopard so it shall not be blown down (out of history)

(the double turns on me with a black look, with a knife)

discernable to the interior eye is my self talking with someone else   One of me sees me there

orbiting the eyes

food of light
flood

the soul with the body's first double

On the stoop from which sleep descends

a word slipped into the folds of sleep :

isicorpus

******

   isicorpus :   the body at its
      most perfect crystal
         (outer shell, crystal)
         (body cavity, crystal)
         (crystal liver, crystal heart, crystal kidney)

         the body at its glass
                  apogee
        about to shatter

******

That was the dream word, and those were the dream words that followed. *Isinglass* is
the waking word suggested
       Is that Isinglass (collagen) (1) *or Isinglass (mineral)* (2)?
******

(2): Isinglass mineral:

as if the body were Muscovy-glass, a mica window to look through
as if the body were a lattice point graph
luxuriating in *birefringence*: a ray of light decomposing
into its ordinary (o-) and extraordinary (e-) ray : if looking through a calcite crystal
we see
the world twice, its ordinary and extraordinary face

the body melts down to its
ordinary bones

*****

(1): Isinglass collagen:

isinglass fining[1] : collagen[2] boiled out
from Beluga sturgeon swim bladders :

      the oldest adhesive[3]

      "has been used to repair experimental incisions in rabbit lungs"

    the cell takes its window-like structure

break it down
boiling skins & sinews of horses
build something new

blancmange you could build
called "shape"

eat the white shape of my face

make it with milk and calf's foot, with hartshorn jelly
with shredded capon, almond, and rosewater

---

[1] "Egg whites, gelatin, isinglass, diatomaceous earth, blood, milk, bentonite, and carbon have all been used as finings," flocculation agents used to clarify wine or beer. *Flocculation:* a solute comes out of a solution in flakes, *flocs.*

[2] *Collagen,* Gr. *kolla* : glue, glue producer.

[3] 8,310-8,110 before present: used for waterproofing & a decorative webbing on human skulls (found in Nahal Hemar Cave, Israel), like an afterlife beehive or hairnet.

*****

(2):

under the o-ray the body will stay
(if looking at the body through a calcite crystal
or if looking at the body through tourmaline
looking at it through quartz or
if you are looking at the body the naked
body through ice) under the o-ray the body
will stay
the body

under the e-ray it will rotate around itself if the crystal
or ice
if you are looking at the body
through ice and you rotate
the ice the body
will cast its double   will describe
its circle
its animal circle
as a ghost

We don't decorate the baby like a house
she decorates us and
she decorates herself

She puts flesh on the future

& the future looks better
& the future looks worse

•   •   •

Many mothers are there a mirror
[to remind us]   not who we are but
what we were   that's why   a mother
can raw the nerves

• • •

of the representatives of concluded humanity
the remnants remain hem-ragged

the stars' hidden points[1] are
embedded in the body

in the patient process each species is engaged in
she undertook to look like herself

"animal again at the end of history"
given back to animal praxis and animal pain

even now (doubleblind) the two or three animals inside
even now (doubleblind) the living animal carrying the mirror-dead the dead
animal inside

---

[1] bipeds, quadrupeds, birds, fish, reptiles
(5 parts of the animal kingdom)
bones, nerves, veins, flesh, skin
(5 natures of the human body)

Downy Rattlesnake Plantain Orchid
(Goodyera pubescens)

how mayonnaise becomes a ghost her
    unruly hue   how we hold
       our hands   whitening the light

roads ruin   in daylight   they
   ruin in the night

my seenless companion air
  seekless there

a blue⌋ sleeve hung between the light
   a seamless sun

now how the afterlife reflects its light
  into the living

•   •   •

ensleeped in the beau silk sleeve
   of youth & love

until sleep becomes so thick it's death

the dreams are mirrors of the day
the days are mirrors of the dream

Each word is a plume feathering the bird

(I'm envisioning a chicken which makes it
edible)

It is late July out on the lake

I put my hands on his shoulders

She puts her hands on my face

Dirt is still stuck to the bone where you sailed in a mammal's purse

Pitched shark body mailed from mother in a leather envelope

In my dream of publishing a face

The body's velvets slide out to publish the face

In the human reproduction exhibit, we turn the body inside out

It's bloody work
to publish a face

In some stories feet will dance without their bodies

•   •   •

in the morning, she is making circle-shadows on my shoulder with her fingers,
claiming

"elbow, elbow"

shoulder, I say, and make a circle on her elbow

shoulder, she says, circling my elbow, why

is your shoulder an elbow she wonders are you an

hour or are you an arm. then I'm a shoulder, pale, and I sing

the dreams are mirrors of the day
the days are mirrors of the dream

in the operating room a corpse is being emptied of its sex, thousands of translucent orange eggs like tobiko scatter out of the body, across the floor . bloated rubbery (the real body we saw floating in the East River?) . the presiding surgeon says, a corpse is ambidextrous a corpse is androgynous look what a corpse can do

• • •

of all the hours piled inside the body
when time finally pulls back from its flesh
the hours tumble   out again

her tiny dress her tiny
tiny death
her dress her hands her death

shows wind a way to colloquy
in a doorway or a corner

or under car wheels, snow spiriting up

the slender and sylphy Hours of the Night, each
of brightly forked tail feathers trailing

unfolds (enfolds)

to put my head
a slipper to a pillow, a satin
slip to sleep on (*pillow my case, stained* gift)

(an *orange rind* is) something
to stun you out of sleep, to
bring trees to your morning
an *orange rind* may fragrance my hours &
draw out the ghost

"I could see my daughter beginning to climb
 hand over hand like a little gold
 animal in the morning sun." Animals are gold & children
 are metal I do not want to continue for I
 do not want my daughter to die. Switch sleepers. Gold
 is a serious color of sleep, like gold smoke breathing through the nostrils
 of the dreamer. Gold leaks up the bridge & hovers
 on the lids of the eyes like small swamps, Cow Hollow. Gold being close to God
 and God being close to Cow is the color
 that never weeps but the sleeper. The strings of the sleeper, golden
 worms emerge
 from the body, tying sleeper to sleep. So
 easily a string snaps, sleeper was flying, drops,
 wakes. They say if you die in a dream you
 die. Why.

in the quiet sleep of animals
from the balcony of a belly
say your speeches
no cow licked you
I do

I began making sketches in my notebook to clarify an experience in which I found my self languageless. In this strange new condition, the outside body was acting like a clock, engaged in a timed performance out of which a product would emerge. The inside body was a body preparing to move from timelessness to time. My brain was a hot, mushy hollow. But I began to think through bodies, and through D'Arcy Wentworth Thompson, about the growth (and decay) of bodies in time, the cohabitation of these two functions. A minute sprouts a cell, an hour an arm. After my daughter was born (had moved into time), time was at a higher premium than ever. I tried sketching portraits of minutes, attempting to contain them within that temporal allocation. Later, I graduated to hours, experimenting with the shape and line of consciousness within the container. My initial plan was not to find poems, but to find time. Soon, I realized, in the hours, that these were poem-drawings. If it will help the reader, I add: the handwritten words were made within the hour and its line-gestures. The typed language below, which appears as a footnote, is the language residue of the experiment. The shaped residue of language is the portion I'm most willing to let clarity represent.

COLOPHON

Body Clock was designed at Coffee House Press,
in the historic warehouse district of downtown Minneapolis.
The text is set in Caslon.

FUNDER ACKNOWLEDGMENTS

Coffee House Press is an independent nonprofit literary publisher. Our books are made possible through the generous support of grants and gifts from many foundations, corporate giving programs, state and federal support, and through donations from individuals who believe in the transformational power of literature. Coffee House Press receives general operating support from the Minnesota State Arts Board, through an appropriation by the Minnesota State Legislature and from the National Endowment for the Arts, and major general operating support from the McKnight Foundation, and from Target. Coffee House also receives support from: two anonymous donors; the Elmer L. and Eleanor J. Andersen Foundation; Bill Berkson; the Buuck Family Foundation; the Patrick and Aimee Butler Family Foundation; Jennifer Haugh; Joanne Hilton; Stephen and Isabel Keating; the Kenneth Koch Literary Estate; Allan and Cinda Kornblum; Seymour Kornblum and Gerry Lauter; Kathryn and Dean Koutsky; Ethan J. Litman; Mary McDermid; Stu Wilson and Melissa Barker; the Lenfestey Family Foundation; Rebecca Rand; the law firm of Schwegman, Lundberg, Woessner, PA.; Charles Steffey and Suzannah Martin; the James R. Thorpe Foundation; the Woessner Freeman Family Foundation; the Wood-Rill Foundation; and many other generous individual donors.

To you and our many readers across the country,
we send our thanks for your continuing support.

Good books are brewing at coffeehousepress.org